HOW TO WRITE LESS, PROFIT MORE

A Rich Adventure in Short Story Self-Publishing

I0486817

HOW TO WRITE LESS AND PROFIT MORE - VERSION 2.0

First edition. February 3, 2021.

Copyright © 2021 Dr. Robert C. Worstell.

ISBN: 978-1393868514

Written by Dr. Robert C. Worstell.

Table of Contents

To all our many devoted and loyal fans:

We produce these stories only for you.

(Be sure to get your bonuses at the end of the book...)

- - - -

Look for addtional versions of this book in print, audio, and course formats. Ask your bookseller for the versions you want - see also the Related Books section at the end.

Prelude

───

HERE'S THE CORE OF this book – test this as you go:

• *You can make more money writing short stories and publishing them weekly than you will writing huge novels that take months to write and another half-month to edit.*

• *You get paid more per page for short stories.* They take less time to write and edit. You spend more on covers, true.

• *But you make it all back when you compile them into anthologies,* particularly if you publish those in print. And that compilation doesn't have to be closely edited, because those books already have been.

• *Meanwhile, short stories enable you to learn your craft and to tighten up your prose.* You can study cliffhangers and learn to write in always-popular serials and series. Which then bring you right back to publishing in thick collections.

The bottom line is that you are going to get more efficient at writing and publishing. You'll start by writing and publishing a short story every week. Every so many weeks, you'll take a bit of time to collate these into a collection and publish that, too.

By the end of a year, you can have something like four dozen short stories and maybe a dozen collections as well. All sitting there, available for purchase from the week they were written. You don't publish two or three times a year. You publish something around 6 dozen times per year.

The rest of this book just explains how that is true, how it can earn you more income for each word you write, and how you can do that just by yourself – with the resources you already have at hand.

But you'll have to test this for yourself.

I've already done my testing. That's why I'm writing it up for you. Because I did write this up before. And people keep buying that book and coming to my website for that out-dated version.

This updated version is more streamlined. Or at least it isn't just based on some marketer's hype – now that I've tested those marketer's claims and found them to contain more hype than proved strategies.

This updated version is based on my own results.

So – let me get out of your way. You've got a lot of testing ahead of you, already...

Is it possible to earn more money working less time?

AND STILL DO ONLY WHAT you *love*?

It is when you ignore the conventional wisdom out there, especially the "Get Rich Quick" guru's.

T. Harv Eker traced his own financial success to a friend of his father, who took him aside during a break in a card game.

Eker had just moved back in with his parents after failing at his *seventh* business and losing everything – *again*.

The advice he got then was very sound: "If you want to get rich, learn what the rich people know. You study what they do."

And Walter J. Stanley was surprised in his study of millionaires, finding that the people who live in those expensive houses usually can't really afford them – all while the millionaires are more than likely living in a neighborhood like your own, under a modest suburban roof or in a small town.

What is a writing success?

THE CORE PREMISE TO this book should have followed: if you want to be a success at writing, study what the successful writers are doing and have always done to make their success. And that's for whatever you consider success is – whether it's making a lot of sales, a lot of take-home income, or just publishing the books they've always known that they would write someday.

The route to failure is simple: *swallow the kool-aid of the self-styled guru's.*

There are tons of books and courses out there, along with webinars and in-person seminars, that will offer to teach you how to "make a 6-figure income from Amazon publishing".

But the only available statistics show that just four-tenths of all the authors on Amazon make more than $50K – which isn't even enough to live on in larger metropolitan areas.

You have to set out what a success is for you. Then study the writers who made that sort of success for themselves.

By studying over 270 books on writing and authorship, some written over a century ago, I narrowed down the really usable books to less than a dozen.

The commonality between these usable ones? They were written by authors who had developed a following by the quality of their writing, and *incidentally* wrote a book (or even a short essay) on what they had learned along the way.

(The worst books? By professors. That phrase comes to mind, however twisted: "Those who can't do, teach – and those who can't teach write textbooks.")

The second worst writing-publishing advice books were written by marketers who had tortured their copywriting skills into writing longer non-fiction or fiction.

How to Fail at Success

ANYONE CAN SIT DOWN with a few hours on their computer and use a search engine to drag up enough material to fill a short ebook they can stuff on Amazon with the right keyword phrases to make it discoverable and price it cheap enough to sell.

And that above is really the core premise of what passes for "conventional wisdom" from the self-styled "guru's".

Most of the "successes" I've seen promoted on the various writing sites, blogs, or forums were of two types. 1) They were marketers who learned how to write. 2) They were writers who learned how to market.

You can find out more about any author by what they are *doing* instead than what made their success. The "big names" I keep hearing about are building and promoting their *courses*. And in those courses, there is very little about the craft of writing – but a lot about the mechanics of getting sales through marketing.

Seriously. The blind are leading the blind.

Advertising Scams

JUST A WARNING SHOT here – in fiction writing especially, there is a literal ton of hype on how you should advertise to get your books discovered. And in the core basic principles, they are right. But what they are preaching you have to take with a grain of salt. There are more people losing their shirt with advertising than are making enough income to make them a living from book sales alone.

One author I studied was the "top-selling author on Amazon" that year. While his books were undoubtedly good, the way he did it was to run ads on Amazon that were profitable. Now, "profitable" means that you at least got one cent more in book-royalties than you paid out in ads. Nowhere did this author ever state how much profit he actually pulled in after he paid off all the personal loans he took out from relatives and friends to pay for his advertising.

Even the most transparent of all authors won't give you enough numerical details to really work out what their take-home profits were. They"ll tell you a rough ad-spend budget, and units sold, but won't do that final breakdown which is more like an IRS tax form. Because: government taxes for one, and secondly is that they'd be picked apart by nay-sayers.

In three years of writing fiction, I can emphatically reveal that "organic" discovery is completely dead, if it's ever been alive. I've done the tests.

Thoreau talked about building that "better mousetrap" where the "world would beat a path to your door".

But Nope. Doesn't happen. (Frankly, he needed to get a cat for that cabin of his.)

It also doesn't happen in non-fiction, where the search engines inadvertently promote your book for you – based on the words in your title, sub-title and blurb text. Also known as "keyword phrases".

Amazon is not your friend.

THEY ARE THE BIGGEST U. S. bookseller. And they are in business to make a profit. So they are paying their "exclusive" authors less and less each year, even though they promote that the total amount distributed as royalties rises every year.

The authors I've followed who were in Amazon's exclusive area have seen their income halved just a few years after they started. Of course, those authors are still making nice six-figures, but they all reported the same *percentage* of lost income.

Amazon's solution to this? They started allowing authors to run ads on the site. Meaning: higher overhead, more money in Amazon's pockets. And the average author still can't make a living from their sales.

For all you spend to get people to your book page on Amazon, that page is also booby-trapped. By one count, there are over 200 links going somewhere else on any single book page on average. *It's easier for someone to click somewhere else than buy your book.*

The reality of it is – ebooks are bringing people to Amazon to buy other stuff while they are there. That idea is called "loss-leaders". And explains why Amazon has set their 70% royalties to a range between 2.99 and 9.99 – so ebooks are encouraged to "race to the bottom" so people can find real bargains. Meanwhile, Amazon punishes the traditional publishers who insist on pricing their ebooks to match their print versions.

To Amazon, both authors and their books are commodities. The more you sell, the more they profit. But if you and your books disappeared tomorrow, then someone else would take your place.

Romance authors are now churning out 300+ page books every year, and pricing them at $2.99 or less, just to keep up with all their competition. So they are having to write constantly so they can have the next book out in the series. (That's called "feeding the beast".) While with the ads they feel they need to run, the mantra is still the same: don't quit your day job.

How do Nora Roberts and James Patterson solve this? Producing an average of around 10 books a year. While Roberts denies getting any writing help (other than publishing and covers) Patterson admits he's more of a chief editor and uses ghost writers and co-authors to "develop" his ideas. They are each running a publishing business. Patterson's background was as an advertising executive, so that shouldn't be any surprise.

The top writers of the pulp magazine days did over a million words a year personally. And that could account for some 80K words per month (or somewhere around 960K words per year, so the math supports those tales) – enough for 12 decent-sized novels in a year. To write 160K-word novels would take two months, etc. Although some were known for cranking out two 30K novelettes in a week when they needed.

A publishing business probably has a better chance at success than an individual "by the pants" writer-publisher. Even though the overhead would be much higher. And that would explain how so few authors make a viable living at this, particularly fiction writers.

Non-fiction writers often use just a few books or a handful to complement their speaking or consultant gig's. And that's in addition to any brick-and-mortar business. Still, that business doesn't live or die by putting all of it's eggs in Amazon's basket.

Because once your account is canceled by Amazon, well, you'd better always have a Plan B to pay your rent or mortgage.

What You Can Get Out of My Three Years of Tests

WE'VE COVERED SOME of the horror stories, and some of the background that went into these last few years of fiction writing.

But the key point is to go back to what you consider your success is.

And that will usually go back to whatever goal you set for yourself.

I set out to write and publish 50 short stories in the first year. This the same goal that Louis L'Amour, Mary Roberts Rinehart, and others made – *write and sell one short story per week.* (Of course, in self-publishing, you are your own acceptance editor.) Other authors also started this way – Ray Bradbury, Isaac Asimov, "Max Brand", Erle Stanley Gardner, Leigh Brackett, and many now lesser-known million-word-per-year authors such as H. Bedford Jones, William Wallace Cook, Lester Dent, and others.

It's a proved approach to learning your craft while you build your backlist of published books. If all those authors made a decent living from it, and later went on to become famous as authors – it must work, somehow.

And I explore the math of why this is so potentially profitable later.

Yes, I did make some income from writing all these books. But my non-fiction books supported all this research.

Meanwhile, in three years, I averaged 50 short stories every year, 158 total. And also over 60 collected anthologies during that time.

What was surprising is that my paperback anthologies sold much better than my short ebooks. (It shouldn't have been surprising, since paper and hardback books have outsold ebooks more than two to one since ebooks ever arrived on the scene.) But the ebook anthologies themselves sold better as well.

Regardless, all that practice in writing resolved itself into habits that I still have today. My imagination now sports a handy, chrome-plated faucet, which can be turned on or off at will. To write now, is simply to sit down and blank the screen of any other windows. A title appears, a blurb of description, and the characters start reciting their dialog faster than I can type.

And I've learned that writing is a great deal of fun. I enjoy it immensely.

So this three-year experiment has succeeded on many levels, and shown me non-monetary wealth I never expected.

I wrote basically two six-hour days a week, proofing and publishing on that last day. Sometimes that 12 hours would stretch over a week at most (or the book would end up needing to be a small novella). But publish I did. Because I had a deadline, and that next story was tapping its foot off-stage, impatient to be in front of that microphone and the spotlight.

Each story was between 6K and 8K on average. Meaning I wrote an average of 84K words of original fiction every year.

This doesn't take into account the 41 non-fiction books I also published during those three years as well.

Having creative fun all the while.

The point here is that anyone can do this. You can start today and have a stable of published books in just a few months.

Or simple sit down and write that one which has been haunting you your whole life up to this point.

All I suggest is that you write it in short parts.

Because it's easier, simpler, and gets you started faster. None of it takes much time. And the potential profit is still there, even if that's not why you're writing – or if it is.

Whatever you decide, heed this final warning:

Test everything you read or hear, especially if it came from me.

Because you won't know if something is true unless you test it. When it's true for you, it's workable. And the ancient Polynesians said it this way: "Truth is as valuable as it is workable."

What you've heard above is my own journey.

What follows is yours.

That Light in The Tunnel isn't Another Train

———

THE FIRST TIME I WROTE about this area, in the first version of this book, I was being lead by the nose, willingly, by a supposed expert who turned out to be another marketer with a pitch. (And it turned out that his "expert" advice only worked if you were writing exclusively for Amazon inside their walled garden.)

He told of this set of readers who were turning to their Kindle to get their reading fix in short doses.

The trick was that these types of readers have always been there. Having an e-reader around (or a smartphone) just started making it easier. Because you can start and stop reading simply.

In fact, I ran across Stephen King describing this in his "On Writing":

> *[B]ooks are a uniquely portable magic. I usually listen to one in the car... and carry another wherever I go. You just never know when you'll want an escape hatch: mile-long lines at tollbooth plazas, the fifteen minutes you have to spend in the hall of some boring college building waiting for your advisor (who's got some yank-off in there threatening to commit suicide because he/she is flunking Custom Kurm-furling 101) to come out so you can get his signature on a drop-card, airport boarding lounges, laundromats on rainy afternoons, and the absolute worst, which is the doctor's office when the guy is running late and you have to wait half an hour in order to have something sensitive mauled. At such times I find a book vital.*

Short stories are just the way you can start to help these people fulfill that want (or in King's world – a vital need).

And short stories have *always* been around to fill that niche – even when they had to be published in printed magazines to get circulated.

O. Henry and Jack London made their living based on just such short stories and later collections of their works.

Or, you could go slightly earlier and find where serials were another approach – each chapter holding the same elements as any good short story. Charles Dickens was known for these more than his longer works when he was getting started.

The collection of short stories is the same as the collection of serial installments into the final book. Jack London's longest work was actually serialized in a magazine first. As was Dickens' monster tome "Great Expectations".

The same approach goes through and through our modern history and culture. People have to live their lives with long hours devoted to less interesting things than reading for education, entertainment, or inspiration.

But – the short snatches of time are when they could pause and let themselves be transported into other worlds and adventures.

Our days, we have a thin electronic wafer in our pocket or purse that contains thousands of stories to lose ourselves in. In earlier days, close to two centuries ago, it was a folded copy of a printed magazine that was getting more dog-eared from frequent stuffings into suit pockets or handbags.

It's just easier and simpler to write shorter.

THE MATH OF THIS IS simple. If you have but a couple of hours per day to write, you can write in short pieces. Some writers with children say that this valuable writing time has to be snatched in half-hour pieces during the day. Between feedings, baths, naps, and playtimes.

Just work it out so you can write short, then publish these short piece on their own, or later compile them into longer works.

The low end of these, established by Apple and Amazon is 2500 words. Children's books can be merely 500 words, but are illustrated every other page. So they fall into the same category as coffee-table photography books.

Each in their own write-ups, Lester Dent and Nelson S. Bond gave their advices of writing 6,000 words as a good base for an adventure story. This was the rough average the pulp magazines wanted in those days. And it still fits well with our modern stories.

If you can only write 500 words an hour, then that's about 12 hours to write a story, or 6 days of writing if you can only spare 2 hours per day. Get up to 2000 words in a morning like Stephen King held himself in his "On Writing", and you've got the essence of a story in three of these mornings.

Here's the other math to take into account:

• 6,000 words per week is 300,000 words per year.

• And thats 6 novels of 50,000 words each (once you collect them up.)

If you can keep that 2K per day up all week, then that's 14K per week, and 700K words per year, and 14 decent novels per year.

Of course, if you write in serials, you can have these as long as you want. All according to how much your imagination will let you stretch that story out.

The typical Romance story is 300 pages, which runs about 300 words in print (slightly less words required in ebook pages). Said 300-page book would then need 90,000 words – meaning you could assemble 3 such novel-lengths in a year, plus a third of the next one.

The point is writing daily. And as you keep this up, that will become a habit.

At the same time, each 6,000 word short story is publishable on its own. You then make some time to get covers and blurbs ready for each story as a book on its own. And you then have your 50 books in a year at one short story each week.

More than that, getting toward 14,000 words per week, then you'll have well over a hundred books in a year.

That's what happened to me the first year. I found myself writing the next story after I finished the first one. So 12,000 words became my usual. And while some stories ran longer, it gave me an average of two published books each week.

Not that I recommend this to you – because I did all my own covers as well. (Graphics art background.) All I'm saying is that it has been done since before you were born.

Want to be known as "that prolific writer"?

IF YOU WANT TO BECOME prolific, it doesn't take more than a few hours each day – at a pace you can afford. You just have to do it regularly, and publish what you write.

Robert Heinlein laid out 5 rules for writing in his essay "On the Writing of Speculative Fiction".

1. You must write.
2. You must finish what you write.
3. You must refrain from rewriting, except to editorial order.
4. You must put the work on the market.
5. You must keep the work on the market until it is sold.

Of course, there is a lot to disagree with in these rules. But these lay down the gauntlet for any short story writer.

- Write regularly.

- Finish writing the story that you started.

- Edit, proof, revise – sure, but don't rewrite the whole thing.

- Get it published.

- Keep it available for purchase, somewhere, always.

That's almost all there is to being prolific.

Both Louis L'Amour and H. Bedford Jones had this advice in addition:

Once you reach "The End", then put in another piece of paper in your typewriter and start the next one.

And *that's* all there is to being prolific. Lots of writing, story after story after story.

Personally, I'd add the point that you should really like doing this. There must be something you enjoy in all this.

Those that don't will find excuses and perfectly good reasons for doing something else.

Some people aren't cut out for the discipline of writing. Others consider they have only that one story in them. Marketers will find themselves gravitating to hyping courses about writing instead of cranking out novels.

All that is fine. Each to their own.

But if you have that one story in you, then get it out to the world. In these days of low-cost publishing, artwork, proofing – there's no reason not to.

On the other hand, more readers are always appreciated as well...

Your choice.

Competition – another needless worry

IF YOU DO WHAT EVERYONE else is doing, of course you'll have competition.

The continuing work of Alex Newton at his K-Lytics.com has probably the best breakdown of short reads and short stories on Amazon in 2015, and updated these in 2017 and then 2019.

The key points he reveals are these:

• About 25% of the total Kindle ebook supply fall into the short reads category (less than 100 pages total, or 25,000 words).

• Only 7% of the books displayed seem to be selling at all.

• While there is more demand per book for longer reads, as shown in higher prices, more is paid *per page* for short reads. While Romance and SF/Fantasy are churning out 300-400 page books, they are getting paid about a cent per page, while short reads for those categories are around 70 pages and are getting 3 cents per page. (See where the title of this book comes from?)

Meaning that you have much less competition and are paid better for the stories you write as they sell.

What takes less time and energy (and money, if you're hiring out proofing) – writing 300 and 400 page novels, or writing the same amount of words into multiple 70-page books?

And guess what – 70-page books are easier to proof and faster to turn out, even with the additional covers, than those big tomes that take at least a third of the year just to write?

(70 page books are just over 17,000 words, so figure about three weeks to write. Or do a trilogy and publish it as three individual 6,000-word books and then also as a set.)

You have a chance at selling all these short works and also the longer ones. If they like your short works, then...

Back to this competition myth: *75% less competition on Kindle when you write shorter works.* And you get paid more per page when they sell. Readers who want longer works will then choose your compiled versions, which are long enough to also appear in print. (Which, remember, consistently out-sell ebook versions.)

Meanwhile, you have a relatively stress-free life of being able to write, proof, revise, and publish one book per week. And every three weeks or so, you compile those into longer works – to then put them up on sale as well.

Of course, when you have enough books, perhaps quarterly or bi-annually, you'll then come out with one of these massive tomes that people like so much.

As an author, you're now in and out of these various short story and novel categories. So a book might sell as part of shorter and longer collections or by itself.

You aren't having to shift gears into proofing and review of that massive tome every four months. Once you've gotten that short story proofed, revised, and published, then it's done pretty much forever. So there isn't any long proofing and editing action required to make a big tome of 300

– 400 pages. Just compile them all together in a sequence that make the most sense to you and your readers.

I can stitch together a book that size in an afternoon. Because I don't have to re-check much once it's all together. I already did all the writing, proofing, and editing needed – when I published it the first time.

Competition by short read category – who cares?

GOING DOWN INTO THE 2019 K-lytics report, we see where Romance has a high sales volume with relatively low competition in the "two hours or more" area (44-64 pages).

So you can see right off what this means. A 6,000 word short story is 24 pages. So two of these (the second being a sequel or prequel to the first) would cover the minimum. Or write a trilogy of stories that are slightly under 6K words. Or one longish story with a short prequel and a short sequel, just to take the total length up to 64 pages. Two or three weeks and it's a done deal.

Writing a 16,000-word story doesn't have to be your first work. That prequel could be a character study, to set the scene. The sequel could be "yeah, but whatever happened to that supporting character after that?"

You're more flexible while writing short.

Do sales by category on Amazon really matter?

THE REASON FOR STUDYING K-lytics isn't so you can pick out all the categories your book should be listed in. The real use is to see in general terms what U. S. readers are looking for. (Recall that Amazon has over 50% of the U. S. ebook market, and more of the paperback sales than any other single bookstore or outlet.)

You **don't** do what's recommended – which is to "write to market."

Never, ever. Ever.

Sure, you put in the "obligatory scenes" that your genre requires. Romances always end with a happily ever after, or a promise of one. Space opera has to be out in space, Westerns have to be out West.

But – you write what you love to read. Always.

That is where you'll do your best. Every time. Every. Single. Time.

Trying to write Romances for Amazon became a problem child because the spammers figured out how to game the system with their cobbled-together super-long pastiches based on the formulaic plot that is common to all Romances.

Then the GRQ (Get Rich Quick) guru's followed by saying that this was the "hot thing" right now (which in their speak means that it's already past its peak and has since been declining in sales.)

If you love reading Romance, then figure out what sub-sub-sub-niche you can write for where people will be able to find your book. And then advertise in that specific, tiny area.

Or – don't. And just write what you specifically love to read.

The rule of thumb is that if you are slogging through your writing, the reader is going to be slogging through your reading.

So maybe you simply don't want to advertise, and just let your book take its chances. Maybe you don't mind having a hobby that pays for itself sometimes.

Because writing also has benefits for your soul. You can examine subject areas that you won't talk about in real life, even with your closest friends or confidants.

Other stupid Amazon tricks you can learn

AND I COULD ALSO GO the SEO route for Amazon, where the term "short stories" is used way more often than any other to find books to read in this area.

Meanwhile, K-lytics assembled a virtual bestseller list of the top 100 short reads titles. And reveal that your page length should be (drum-roll, please) – 74 (or just over 18K words – three 6K short stories).

There are categories that aren't short reads, but may be. "Literature & Fiction- Short Stories" is a main category. The books in it may or may not be short reads. (Because novellas are short stories – they certainly aren't novels.)

Meanwhile, there are several sub-markets where there are less than a thousand titles to compete with.

The reason I call these stupid tricks is that these are so precise and esoteric to only work on Amazon. And I'll go over in more detail why being exclusive to Amazon, or even basing your marketing solely on Amazon will just drive you bonkers. Because Amazon starts running your life, giving you another boss you don't need. And you'll start second-guessing everything about whatever sales you're getting – because no one knows the Amazon algorithms exactly, except Amazon.

K-lytics is good to give hope that we can figure out some broad applications for what is working there. And then apply these to our books in terms of audience expectations, and our keywords that will work on Amazon and everywhere else as well.

Note again, as I said above, advertising expense is apparently required to get your fiction book discovered with any speed on Amazon. Just the way they've set it up.

There are better ways coming up. Just like you'll have more enjoyment out of writing what you love to read.

Publishing and marketing your books can be enjoyable, too.

Learning Your Craft With Short Story Writing

———

SHORT STORIES ARE A great way to try things out, and to study craft points used in long novels, but can be shoe-horned into a short story as well.

You have only a little space in short stories.

Sure, you can take as much room as you like – but consider this: Short stories are great practice for writing longer pieces. Consider that every chapter in a long book is like a magazine serial. So you have to grab the reader and transport them in a few seconds, then keep them totally engrossed until the very end.

The end of that chapter then has a cliff-hanger that encourages them to turn the page and get into the next one.

All of these you can practice with your short stories.

Consider this: your short story has an end. And then a final chapter puts the same characters into another situation – which they can only resolve by buying your next book in that series.

Ooh – so dastardly. But figure that you're writing in series (which readers want) and when you collate this next collection of all the books in this series, it will hang together quite well with out a lot of editing.

Also, people want serial books. So your short stories then just flow from one to the next. And readers who identify with your characters will then find more adventures to help them get distracted from the obnoxious "real world" that surrounds us. You just promised that.

All the other points, about staring in the middle of the action, of using all the senses in your descriptions to bring your reader right into the story, leaving them in the middle of something at every chapter or section break – all of these can be practiced with every single story you write.

Some smart tricks for savvy short story authors

1) WRITE IN PEN NAMES for different main genres or story structures.

The main story structures are: Adventure, Mystery, Romance, Redemption, and Non-Fiction. Each of these have a physical structure of what happens when. Physical in terms of what has to be written at what point of the story. Each have required elements that readers expect. And writing in each single structure to begin with gives you good practice.

Within certain genres, like Mystery, there are widely different sub-genres that have their own particularities (ghost mysteries are quite different than detective-mysteries.) So using a pen name for your studies in and around these different structures and genres gives you a bit more latitude than jumping between the structures with a single pen name.

Using one pen name per story structure tells the reader to expect a certain story when they open it up. That is why genres were created, to begin with. And why Science Fiction was the first genre to break away from general adventure fiction.

When you want to practice in a different main structure, then adopt an additional pen name. Romance has an overall formulaic plot, but the great part of this is being able to practice shifting with your settings and characters.

2) Co-authors with multiple pen-names.

Of course when you are writing a mystery with a heavy romantic sub-story-arc, then you can have your two pen names on the book cover and listed as authors.

What this will do is to promise fans of each of these authors that they will be getting what they expect.

You practice with various stories until you are confident you can write a straight story structure. And then you start running the other story structure elements in, side-by-side, with the first. So the mystery has some crime committed at the beginning that also forces the two lovers to work together in spite of the fact they had freshly broken up just before the story starts.

While they solve the crime's mystery, they also have to solve their own relationship meanwhile. And while you know they will solve them both, the many twists and red herrings keeps you wondering how.

Why "Write Short and Narrow, Publish Long and Wide" Works

———

AGAIN, AMAZON ISN'T your friend. They exist to get as much of your money as they can. And they'll do about anything they can get away with to accomplish that.

They have over 50% of the U. S. ebook market, and more than that with print books.

However, Kobo has 50% of the *International* market, including the U. S. Let that sink in for awhile.

While the U. S. market has leveled off as far as expanding ebook consumption, Europe has continued to grow. Amazon has been working to get into those markets, but Kobo has already been there for some time in most of these countries.

Meanwhile, Kobo *only* does ebooks. Another thing to sink in.

Kobo has *real* people curating their books and recommending them. Their job depends on picking books that will sell well.

As covered, ebooks are a loss-leader for Amazon to get them into all the other stuff they sell.

Itunes book sales are an also-ran to their gizmo's.

Barnes & Noble continues to be anyone's guess.

Meanwhile, there are book outlets in many other countries, especially Indonesia where English-language books are in demand.

The math of Amazon Exclusivity

WHILE AUTHORS ARE EXCLUSIVE to Amazon, they don't know what they are missing from other sales. "But I am global!" is the retort. Yes, but not anywhere near what you *could* be – is the reply.

The key point about being only in one huge store is that you are just another commodity as an author and so are your books.

Whatever Amazon changes affects you drastically, one way or the other. If you ever somehow get your account canceled – well, again, where's that day job?

Anecdotally, authors who publish wide report that Amazon is still 50% of their income, but now they are making 25% more (on average) than they were on Amazon alone. They are now making less from Amazon, but the other 50% of their income has more than made up for that change.

One factor in this is local demands across the globe are different than U. S. demands. So your book can sell like hotcakes in a particular country or region, but tank in others.

I've had Amazon bow to a false DMCA complaint and refuse to sell my ebook or its print version. Meanwhile, that same book sold everywhere else. Years later, I did a revision and it started selling on Amazon right off. Slightly different title, same meta-data. Lots more material inside. And Amazon also started selling the paperback.

Had I only published that book on Amazon, I would have missed out on those other sales meanwhile, completely.

Aggravating aggregators

I'VE TRIED EVERY AGGREGATOR service there is. These companies get a slice from getting your books into all possible book distributors. They truly take your book global, to one degree or another. They have different operating bases.

Draft2Digital is quite innovative and for the U. S. market, they are the best. They also have started a Print On Demand service which converts your ebook into paperback, which expands your sales. They accept no public domain books.

PublishDrive is out of Hungary and works a great deal of Europe's smaller book distributors, as well as the main U. S. book outlets. They also don't accept public domain books.

StreetLib is out of Italy and has all the main U. S. book outlets, and a different set of European and Eastern book distributors. They are the only aggregator right now that will accept public domain.

While you can use all three of these, you have to look out for duplication. Publish Drive allows you to set up scripts that will put a hold on certain outlets when you publish.

Other aggregators aren't recommended.

Lulu has always had their ebooks as an add-on for the self-publishers who use their print-on-demand services. They recently started a policy of charging to get your book distributed globally. As well as a minimum of a dollar charged on all books in their own bookstore. And that dollar goes to Lulu – your commission is based on how high above that you set your price. There is no such thing as free there. They do have the best POD service and the oldest. So that's what you use them for. But your ebooks will get better service for lower cost somewhere else. Oh, and they also don't distribute public domain outside their little U. S. ebook storefront.

Ingrams has pricing on their mind as well. You can do POD there, but they have both a set up fee and revisions fee – *plus* an annual fee to keep your book in print. Their ebook operation has some different fees and policies that are a distraction. Ignore. (The reason you hear so much about them – they offer an affiliate commission for the first purchase by new authors.)

Smashwords is probably the oldest aggregator. And if you start there, that's great. No public domain or private licensed right (PLR). And every ebook has to have a "smashwords edition" notice on it's copyright page.

There are other aggregators and POD services, but nothing worth recommending.

Amazon's POD services aren't bad. But when they have access to all your digital files, it just sets you up for a greater chance that your account can be dinged for something. I prefer to use Lulu or Draft2Digital to push my print books there. I also use aggregators to publish my ebooks there. I've been burned more than once (can you tell?)

Where Long and Wide really shine

- **Publishing short** is writing short stories where you can perfect your craft.

- **Publishing narrow** is to limit yourself to specific sub-genres to learn your craft.

- **Publishing long** is combining these into various anthologies and collections.

- **Publishing wide** is getting to all possible online and physical book distributors on the planet.

PUBLISHING WIDE IS also getting into all possible formats. Paperback, Hardback (see Lulu), audiobook (see Findaway through Draft2Digital) and courses for non-fiction (I am happy with Vidnami [AFFLINK] for creating videos.)

The point of these extra formats is that you'll get additional sales because no two readers have the exact same preferences for getting their materials. And especially in non-fiction, readers will be interested in getting multiple versions of the same content.

If you proof your book by reading it aloud, this can give you an audiobook. That same audio can be used to build the course videos. You'll have to learn to edit your audio, but that's a comparatively short learning curve. A free program called "Audacity" runs on every computer platform.

The general advice is then: **First publish short and narrow, later expand to publishing long and wide.**

Courses, the Final Frontier

THERE IS MORE TO CREATING courses and hosting them, but the point here is that Amazon doesn't own any course platforms at this writing. Meanwhile, it's reported by a couple of entrepreneurs I follow that they make 100 times the income (royalties) on any course that they did on the same ebook or even print version. That is a self-hosted course, or using some provider like Thinkific or Teachable.

There are several good marketplaces for courses, such as Udemy and Skillshare – but their real use is in uploading mini-courses which excite people and lead them back to your main course on another provider. Similar to what you have to do with lead magnets in the back of your Amazon books to get them onto your mailing list.

You're next question is: what are you going to do with all this data?

The "Eyeball" Marketing Strategy for Self-Published Books

———

(An excerpt from "Publish. Profit. Independence."[1])

THE SIMPLICITY OF EBOOK sales can be simply stated:

Get Your eBook in Front of as Many Eyeballs as Possible.

But it's not all that simple.

Sure, there are at least 7 main outletsfor ebooks. (And there's another 5 or 6 additional outlets as well...)

No one outlet has any given set of eyeballs in a monopoly. As a matter of fact, at no time can any one of them claim they have all ebook readers under their spell. The closest they can get is this paraphrase from old Abe Lincoln:

You can reach some of the readers most of the time,

You can reach most of the readers some of the time,

But no ebook outlet (or author) can reach most of the readers *most* of the time.

Added to this:

Poor marketers only try to reach some of the readers some of the time. (That's why they're still poor...)

How to reach as many eyeballs as possible

ONE TRICK IN THIS IS that **no given set of people agree on how they like their content served up to them.**

We are starting out with ebooks - most people would still rather read printed books. There's also audiobooks. With digital downloads, these are becoming ever more popular, especially for commutes. On top of that, there's also video versions that can be generated from the same audio. As well, the text can be converted to PDF's and slideshow presentations. And there are packages with combinations of all of these, like you can post on Gumroad, and some service providers such as iAmplify. Meanwhile, there is at least one ebook publisher who allows you to package A/V files with your ebook – Leanpub[2]. (They also encourage you to build courses there.)

This gives a new twist to the old phrase: *Write Once, Publish Many Ways...*

- Write once,

- publish as many ways,

- in as many formats,

- to as many eyeballs

- as possible.

ebooks - The modern ebook author needs to realize that to reach the maximal amount of people viewing your work, you're going to have to be on all possible distribution lines - not just stick with Amazon. There's 6

---

2. http://leanpub.com/

other outlets who want to host your content - and they all reach different readers.

You want to translate (port) your text into multiple formats. Smashword ports your content to multiple formats - all written. epub, mobi, PDF, plus another half-dozen versions for different readers. Leanpub and Draft2Digital only covers PDF, ebub, mobi.

Audio - Then you have audiobooks. Of course, there's ACX which gets you into Audible, Amazon, iTunes. Better have your best show on there - they have serious quality standards. But you also have to realize that simple podcasts by the author are also in demand. Particularly as a bonus. Findaway (which you can access through Draft2Digital) will syndicate your audiobook to a huge variety of outlets outside of Amazon in addition to Amazon itself. [*Update*: you can also post your audio book as "spoken word albums" and distribute as a CD through CDBaby...]

Video - iAmplify gives you a marketplace where you can host your videos. Of course, you can put previews on the major and minor video sites as well. (Use your audio as a soundtrack, then add in powerpoint visuals built on the outline of your text. Or use Vidnami as a higher-end resource.)

PDF's - For promotion, PDF previews can be posted on all the doc-sharing sites, which will bring your site traffic. Many powerpoint-viewing sites take PDF's as well. Scribd hosts PDF's.

Graphics - And then, there are always creating infographics to promote your content, based on the content itself. Pinterest, Flickr, etc. love these. As social media, these take longer to get traction, but if you're publishing regularly, the covers can go there as promotion. Infographics are time consuming, covers you already have.

Your Bottom Line - The trick is to have your money-making backend sites and your promotional sites for generating traffic, search engine ranking, etc. There's going to be a balance.

This is again the whole point of writing. An avid fan base will boost sales and get the ebook outlet algorithms working in your favor.

By contrast, *low-selling ebooks are mostly condemned to that forgotten pile by those algorithms*, it seems especially with Amazon. All outlets have their own versions. Only Amazon really seems to value reviews, for instance. (Reviews have been proved to have little to do with actual purchase, higher is who originally told them about the book.) Low-cost books can get you opt-in's where free book seekers tend to only want more free books. You want people who have some skin in the game.

Meanwhile, I have *several* dozen books on other outlets (who aren't as restrictive on submissions) and know these same books routinely sell in good percentages. But no two outlets have the same audience. Some books I've put up on iTunes don't sell well on Kobo. Barnes & Noble is always an unknown quantity.

Backbench - The point in profitable publishing is to have a *deep* back-bench. The most successful authors have *dozens* of books up there.

I found that it's far more profitable to be a publisher than a writer. So I look for books which are under-marketed (which are easy to find in the public domain and in PLR) - then put them up with appealing covers and good descriptions, then publish them as widely as possible. Some sell well, others don't.

The trick is that for a few hours' work per book, I have quite a few which sell routinely for me. *And these will be selling for me from here on out.* I can then take these and market them further with additional versions, and Search Engine Marketing by providing a back-up website, previews on doc-sharing sites and Bittorrent, etc. I can also use that base popularity to generate extra sales by creating audiobooks and videos based on that proven seller.

Also, I can go back and review the non-sellers to see if something needs to be tweaked in their cover, description, or preview.

So that's my own algorithm, after a fashion.

It starts with having a ton of books up there, on as many outlets as possible, in as many formats as possible. This is now being expanded by being able to collect emails into lists, and offering that audience the alternative books they may have been missing. While this is still in its infancy, I can see this is the best route to leveraging all the above into some serious income.

Again, publishing pays more than writing. But the best writing will make publishing simpler and more profitable.

Remember: Eyeballs drive profits.

Marketers & Writers – Scammers & Dupes

THERE ARE TWO TYPES of people who become "successes" in self-publishing: Marketers who learn to write, and Writers who learn to market.

Success is in quotes as most of the ballyhoo about what constitutes "success" is just that. Most contend it's exaggerated amounts of money. Napoleon Hill mentions 12 different types of riches. A sufficient income is only one of them. The last one on his list.

Look up the "guru's" and what their past history is, and you'll most usually find they were marketers first. One example is the brand-name writer Patterson. He is an advertising-executive-turned-writer. His name has become a brand for a publishing business. Publishes about 10 big books a year or more. Good for him.

Almost all the rest of these "guru's" are primarily marketers at heart. Their hype is intense. One latest approach is to have you pay inordinate amounts of money (about $2 grand) to get hand-held for your first 90 days – just so you can get through your first novel. You'll find the 90-day rule is also held in MLM, where the enthusiasm can only be held for that long until the real world gives you enough feedback to question everything.

Meanwhile, it takes you 30 to 60 days to get through that course.

Can you finish a novel in those last 30 days? Sure – it's called National Novel Writing Month, happens every year, and has a great support section. But it's free.

Fiction writers might have it worst. When you look up the perennial bestsellers, you'll find that all the "overnight" sensations labored for 5-10 years before they "made it big". And often produced that many major-length novels during that time. Average was 1-2 novels per year, about 150K words each year. And it doesn't matter what they credit for their breakthrough, they all have generally the same amount of work to get it.

But ideally, any writer should be able to have their writing output support their writing practice.

The last report of any worth in this area about successful fiction writers (the now defunct authorearnings.com) says that 0.4% of those writing on Amazon make more than $50K per year. (Which is a third of what you need to earn in NYC to live on as an individual. Not so out here in the great unwashed Midwest.)

Writers simply write.

IT'S IN THEIR GENETIC makeup, probably. That they can get paid for the pleasure they get out of writing is an extra benefit.

Those who have any mention of saving time and/or getting money in any headline are generally scammers, IMHO. If you study the *classic* copywriters, you'll find they don't recommend anything like that.

Now, down to bare-bones business.

Here's four key points to making your books earn you support:

1. Writers starting out today should use an aggregator to get their work published wide. Concentrating on Amazon only puts that company in charge of your income. And authors who are only in Kindle Select/Unlimited saw their incomes halve since KU was first set up. And their payouts continue dropping every year. (While Amazon has 50%

of the U. S. Market, Kobo has 50% of the International ebook market, which is still expanding while the U.S. market has plateaued..)

The overall best aggregator to start with is Draft2Digital. Followed closely by PublishDrive and Streetlib. They all have great internal programs to take your rough work and turn it into a decent ebook. D2D is also getting into print publishing, which is still where more sales are happening than ebooks. PublishDrive and Streetlib get your books into more international markets as well as the "Big Four" of Apple, Kobo, B&N, Amazon.

2. The model for authors is "Content Inc." by Joe Pulizzi. It talks from a non-fiction view, but the basics are the same for fiction.

Writing non-fiction is easier to make a decent income from, since the prices are generally a lot higher, and the markets there are vertically-integrated – since readers in these niches tend to buy more of the same in different versions. And they review and restudy the books they get. (Fiction genres are way too broad and overpopulated. While those readers are usually only interested in one-off entertainment and consumable books.)

Fiction ebooks are super-saturated on Amazon and most online ebook distributors. Waaay too much competition. So listening to people who say to "follow the leaders" in these areas are smoking something potent. Read Pulizzi and you'll see writers need to differentiate themselves and select a very, very, very narrow niche they can succeed in.

3. People should go ahead and pull some earlier paper or long essay they wrote and slap a self-made cover on it (Canva is a good resource). Then self-publish under a pen-name. That gets "being a published author" out of their system.

That process takes a few hours out of an afternoon, but could be accomplished in 30 minutes.

And all your work gets better from there.

Then they need to start learning what makes readers really turn pages. What readers think is valuable. Meanwhile, those authors-in-training need to churn out and publish tons of stuff. Who cares if most of it isn't bought the second you publish? Because it won't be, for the most part. Discovery is a long process for an unknown author. But along the line, writers develop habits of being able to get inspired at any time, and to write regardless of everyone and everything around them. They become content producers. In. Spite. Of. And they'll soon have dozens, if not hundreds of books to their credit, pen names or not.

Again, they are constantly learning to improve their craft, purposely making every book better than the last. Someone said that the first million words are practice. No one ever said someone wouldn't like to buy and read your practice works.

Now, if authors want to get decent support from the content they are producing, then have them study Pulizzi. Meanwhile, they are having fun. If not, then maybe they should be doing something else with their time. Because: what's the point, then?

Like farming, writing is a lot of hard work that has to be done for hours every day and week. You don't get recognized for much. But **the rewards are beyond compare if you are following your bliss.** (And that last sentence should be at the beginning of point 3.)

4. Conventional wisdom is like free advice - worth exactly what you pay for it. And as in belly buttons, everyone has at least one they can talk about to whoever will listen.

People, and especially authors starting out, should develop a healthy skepticism about conventional wisdom. (Look this phrase up on quotations sites and you'll see the digital eye-roll this subject gets.)

Learn to accept recommendations tentatively - for testing only. In most cases, you'll wind up doing what your gut already told you is right - at the beginning. (A well-functioning gut is a marvelous thing - but listening to it and making sense of what it's saying takes a whole lot of practice to get any good at utilizing it fully.)

———————

I AGREE THAT PEOPLE can use help getting started. In my own curmudgeonly way, I give out a lot of advice - some of which people buy in book form.

And since I've been publishing since 2006, I've been willing to try many things. Bought a lot of courses. Learned to sieve through the nonsense. Unfortunately, it turned out to be about 95% nonsense. Most seemed decent at first. Lots of good ideas. But the results didn't prove them out. And in going through their material since, I see that it's mostly how to market your books. Very little on writing real quality material – they just emphasize turning out good-looking schlock that people will consume. Most of their "marketing" material is about gaming Amazon's algorithms.

You'll hardly find any marketer-turned-fiction-writer who produces fiction to actually list his titles. While writers who learn marketing want you to buy into their backlist, as you'll want to buy them all.

Hiding your writing because they are marketing experiments and testing is painful.

Writers should be courageous. Sit down and examine the really big ideas with your prose. Study why the top 100 of Gutenberg.org change very little, but keep getting downloaded tens of thousands of times every year. In that list, you'll see what really great fiction is. And why the dozen or so non-fiction really stand out. All mostly without marketing and well after their authors have passed.

If a writer wants to start writing, there are two books that are regularly recommended:

- **Stephen King's "On Writing"** and

- **Dorothea Brande's "Becoming A Writer"**.

Because they talk to the writer about his *craft* and *writing habits*, not the ever-changing world of how to get something published.

Another interesting book is

- **"This Fiction Business" by H. Bedford-Jones.**

All three of these authors were successes *first* before they ever wrote about writing - and those are the best types of books to study in this area. There's only about a dozen of truly successful writers who wrote about writing, so it's a short list.

Otherwise, the best teacher about writing is doing. If someone wants to write fiction, get them to follow Louis L'Amour, Ray Bradbury, Mary Roberts Rinehart, Erle Stanley Gardner (plus too many more) and write a short story every week for a year. At the end of that time, they'll have a good grasp of how to write and all the discipline that goes with it. If they quit writing, that says something, too.

Writing daily blog posts would help in non-fiction. Especially if you then edit and publish them as a book when you get around 12K written. That will then teach a non-fiction writer about having a content calendar and how to write in a certain direction, toward exploring and explaining something valuable.

The opposite is how marketers first approach writing. In their case, it's all where the "profitable" niches are – and what keywords and marketing approaches will get the biggest "buy in" from consumers.

LOOK:

Writers write.

Marketers market.

Scammers scam.

Dupes – well, there's one born every minute.

The trick is that when writers learn marketing, they quit being dupes. Because now they know how they've been used.

And this takes us back to the moral principle of "treating others as you'd like to be treated." For dedicated writers, this is producing valuable books that transport readers from the first line. Marketing and promotion is just letting readers know your incredibly-written books exist.

Sure, find good books and courses on book marketing. Study them. Devour them. Just be sure to check out that marketer's backlist of published works. Test everything they say – starting with what I've told you here.

(PS. My books are linked in the back – and are published almost everywhere.)

9 Key Lessons From A Year of Pulp System Writing

(from "How I Survived My First Year of Fiction Writing[1]")

I SAT OUT AT THE BEGINNING of 2018 to write fiction short stories every week, following the footsteps of Louis L'Amour, Jack London, Mary Roberts Rinehart, Robert Heinlein, Ray Bradbury, and many others. Their general consensus was that achieving the target of 50 short stories was the first step.

I ended up finding that writing at the million-word-per-year level of Erle Stanley Gardner and H. Bedford-Jones (as well as several other pulp-method writers from the 20's to 50's) is actually easier than it seems. There are some caveats, but not very many.

This is my third boil-down of these lessons learned – this time to take it back to a bullet-list and make everything more accessible.

Here's some statistics right off, to give you the production summary as of Week 48:

- 125 original books written and published.

- 27 of these were anthologies

- 2 were full novels (50K plus)

- 96 were individual short stories (at least 2500 words plus, usually 6-8K)

---

1. https://calm.li/FIrstYearFiction

- 637,533 words in single fiction books

- added a typical base of 3400 +/- subscribers to my active list (starting from 0)

- total words published on paid platforms were 2,057,564 (as the short stories were published on their own and also as part of anthologies.) And this doesn't count fiction words also published on free platforms of my own site, Medium, and Wattpad. (It also doesn't count non-fiction blog posts and books.)

And this is just posted here so those who "need" to know I'm walking my talk can have some statistics they can dispute. Otherwise, feel free to ignore this self-congratulatory back-patting.

(*Note*: at week 52, this became 100 original short stories written and published, 38 anthologies compiled and published. Just for 2018.)

"No One School Has All the Teachers"

THIS IS AN OLD ORIENTAL saying (Japanese, if not even earlier) that describes the state of advice out there about how to write, as well as how to publish. I assembled 227 books on the writing craft, then narrowed these down to less than 20 worth really studying. But none of those had all the answers. They only had answers for themselves and their own production systems. And when I took their lessons and tested them, I only assembled a method of writing that worked for me.

You Can Only Compare Yourself With Yourself

OTHER PEOPLE HAVE WHAT works for them. Getting down on yourself because you haven't already cracked 6- or 7-figures of income helps no one. That is the typical problem with many courses about writing and publishing books – they keep touting the "million-dollar" results – and seldom tell about the quiet successes of people simply enjoying their writing and getting some income from it – enough to at least pay for their expenses (or not.) And I made about as much at the end of this year as I was at its beginning. Because I was working on the writing habit, not the income habit. (And these are both habitual mindsets you train in over time.)

Writing is Regular Work – Regular Action Forms Habits

I SET OUT TO WRITE at least one, and possibly two stories each week – and publish them as well. Some weeks I wrote zero. Some weeks I published nearly 10 books. The average was two original fiction books per week. Every couple of months, at least, I collected these up and published them as anthologies. And they generally sell better than the individual books – as a single title. Through this, I developed my own systems for writing, and getting the inspirations I needed. Now they are ingrained as habits. (If it takes 28-40 days to build a habit, what does 196 days give you?)

Prolific Writing is Easy – Making a Living At It is Harder

I HAD TO CHANGE MY target of 50 short stories at about week 23. Because I was about to pass it. One of the first steps I took was to round up everything I had written as fiction and publish it. All under pen names. Wasn't that much. A couple of NaNoWriMo wins. Several flash fiction pieces. And then I got steadily to work writing. After that 23rd week, I resolved to write and publish 2 stories per week. I'd set that up earlier as a solution to getting out from under the "Feeding the Beast" syndrome some authors have experienced with Amazon. But then I found it was a great deal of fun to help these stories come to life. The joy of writing kept me going. Meanwhile, my existing books (mostly non-fiction) kept bringing me enough income to more than cover my bills – without having to pay for advertising.

Writing is All Long-Haul Work – "Overnight Success" is Just More Fiction

LOOK UP THE BACK-TRAIL of any successful author and you'll be able to find a decade or more of work perfecting their craft and setting up their life to support their writing. All you hear about in the press is the last year or so where it started paying off. So you can't listen to these "bally-hooed" successes. Again, you have to compare yourself with yourself. Did you write more this year than last? Get more published? Earn more income? Your own analysis will tell you where you can improve. Stories about others can be inspiring – but don't take them as Gospel. You can only harvest what you plant. And that harvest is more likely a decade or more off. The second best time to start is now. Look up the "prolific authors" on Wikipedia and you'll find them mostly investing several decades at writing. Several. Decades.

Enjoy What You Write And So Will Your Readers

THIS ONE DATUM HAS come up over and over. If you find yourself grinding at writing something, or bored with it – that is also coming through your writing. The only valid reason to write is because you enjoy it. People who try to "make a lot of money" at this never last. It's just too labor intensive. There are no real short-cuts to creating great fiction. So enjoy all you do. If you're having fun, and enjoy re-reading your own stuff, then your real fans will like it too. Reviews mean nothing except to Amazon. Read what you like to get inspiration to write what you like. Then the readers who like your stuff will find it – somehow. At least they won't put it down when they eventually discover it. Best advice I've heard on this is: "*Write what you want to read.*" And then you'll be writing for the best idea of an "avatar" you could find.

Writing is Learned by Writing – Lots of It

THAT'S THE SHEER BOTTOM line. The biggest breakthroughs I've had personally was studying all these courses and craft books – *then throwing them all away*. Once you've internalized (testing these ideas for yourself) then you'll be able to just sit down and write. You'll know if the story is going anywhere. By your own gut feeling and interest the writing coming out of your fingers (or through your auto-transcriber program.) But there is no substitute to writing on a regular basis – and working to make every story better than the last.

Sure, some authors can crank out 20K words per week, and output a million words per year. Not very many of us. Most writers have their day jobs. Many still write in retirement at the same pace they used to write on a part-time basis. I've been blogging and journaling since the late '90's. So writing "straight ahead" with no plot *per se* was more natural to me. But I had some two decades of scratching words out on paper and in digital as a built-in habit when I sat down to just concentrate on writing fiction. The surprise was that it wasn't hard work – but it was enjoyable work. And my stories are much, much better now than when I started. But the "writer's voice" I use is very similar to the one I write my blogs with. Of course, now I know how to make my non-fiction blog posts more interesting to read... Just took a year of dedicated fiction writing to discover how.

Follow and Emulate Perennial-Selling Books, not "Bestsellers"

ABOUT 10 YEARS AFTER Louis L'Amour started writing professionally, he was told that none of his books had ever gone out of print. There are a large handful of writers through history who have achieved this. "Max Brand", Robert E. Howard, Robert Heinlein, Shakespeare, Arthur Conan Doyle, and others are in this small number. Those have set the high bar to reach. History doesn't care about "NYT/ USA Today Bestseller Lists" or even more temporary "Amazon bestsellers".

Look up Gutenberg.org's top 100 lists. Read these authors. Dissect their best books. Test those methods for yourself. Then all this talk about online advertising and "book launches" will fall into perspective.

The first and oldest advice I've heard repeated about successful writing is this: *"Write A Damn Good Book."* All the clues are there in those perennial sellers. Maybe the language needs to be modernized – like "Romeo and Juliet" became "West Side Story". Study the books that live forever and yours might, too.

Stories Are Out There Begging to Be Brought to Life

STEPHEN KING TELLS briefly about this in his "On Writing" – where he says the stories write themselves. Chris Vogler mentions the idea that stories are alive in the appendix to the later editions of his "Writer's Journey." I've found that inspiration is unlimited. The more you practice using your imagination, the better you get at it. The more you write, the easier it is to find the words and phrases you need. Once you train your inspiration to accept the stories that are talking at you all the time, then you can help them come to life. (And then be prepared for them to queue up waiting for you.) All the possible plots have probably already been written. But a plot doesn't make a story. The story is from the characters. For me, it was getting the idea of all the characters in a story sitting down at a long table for a script read-through. And I was the only one in the room who didn't have a copy of that script. Sure, as they went, they'd suggest changes as they interacted with each other. And I would often (if another character didn't) ask them to "cut to the chase" and keep the pace moving. If I was getting bored from too much dialogue or winded explanation of settings, so were my readers. Just let the stories write themselves – but "ride herd on them" as you have to.

And So?

THERE IS NO ONE-SENTENCE summary for this, each of these lessons have their own action plan to implement.

If I were to tell you one set of datums to boil even these down it would be these:

• Sure, read this book. Test everything. Then throw it out if it doesn't work for you.

• Write your own stories the very best you can. Make each one better than any you've written before.

• Work at your own pace.

• Be true to yourself and your stories.

How to Build a Profit-Making Permanent Writing Habit

(from "How I Survived my First Year of Fiction Writing")

AS I WRITE THIS, HAVING just looked up my last two months of fiction writing production, I discovered that I produced at National Novel Writing Month (NaNoWriMo) writing volume for each of the two prior months, and then again in the first three weeks of November.

Meaning: I'd just developed a habit of writing roughly 12.5K words per week for 60 days, where a habit takes from 28-40 days on average to instill.

Why listen to me? I've already summarized what I've accomplished in a year of writing, and the total for the next two years in addition. You can see if you can write and publish that much in a year, let alone 10 months. Yes, I've gotten some sales, too. The rub? *Each of those books cost me nothing to produce.* So all the sales I get are all pure profit. The rest is just letting people know that these books exist so they can buy their own copies.

How did I do this?

SET GOALS – my model is to write, proof, and then publish short stories in that week. So I was intending to write at least two short stories each week, of about 6K each.

Hold myself accountable – Each Monday, I filled out a blog post that started with the key metrics I needed to track in order to be successful. Sometimes I fudged in order to wrap up my publishing on Monday, so that post wouldn't happen until Tuesday. But the vast majority did "hit publish" on Monday.

Focus on the work – by having these metrics, I could start to see common patterns of when I was successful. One of those is to simply blank the screen(s) of everything else. No distractions. All I would have open were one screen (Calibre) that shows the cover and marketing hook for that book. The other screen was a simple text editor. If I needed a browser to look something up, then I'd do that and immediately minimize it again.

Do my writing first – this still haunts me. If I just "check" my email, it will take me into all manner of rabbit holes. So my best success is when I blank the screens last thing at night when I leave for bed.

Play catch up after meal times, away from my work space. Using my smartphone to do most of my email, and all my curation work is simply done in my living room easy chair as a matter of a few minutes after each meal.

Ignore social media – a key rule. Social media is fake. Burns your time with nothing to show for it. How many of those "friends" buy your books, or you can really trust with your life? Some of these are rumored to sell *some* books, but never enough to earn you a living at it. No perennial bestselling book out there depends on social media for squat. Just the pan-flashers. I remove all the unnecessary apps from any smartphone device I have. Don't visit social media, only syndicate there. (Only one of them is an actual activated smartphone, the others are all largish phablets as remote handheld Android computers that connect through my local wi-fi. And all Wal-Mart Black Friday Specials.)

Proof on a smartphone device and _only_ revise those points – I use an ereader app that allows highlighting. Then I go back through just those edits and fix them. The first proof is making sure the structure is correct, with all the needed chapter headings in place, and spell-check done. Using a small screen allows me to read every single word, and catch 98% of the rest of the errors. I then will publish through D2D and do a third (or fourth) proof, correcting and uploading a new version. And if I find myself distracted by a sentence or word, I'll highlight it and correct it. I should be able to read right through a book and keep interested the entire time – even if I know what I wrote and how it's going to turn out. And I should enjoy that book every time. I've only ever thrown one story away because it wasn't any good – then rewrote it from scratch immediately. And proofed and published that week.

Learn you craft well beforehand – I spent around two years studying fiction writing itself. And I still keep my eyes open today for more tips and tricks – as long as they align to the successful principles and patterns I've already distilled. I bought way more courses than I needed and kept studying with people until I wasn't learning any more – or was finding that I needed to correct their erroneous opinions as much as I was learning anything new. And I still have a stack of books on writing that I've scraped from all sorts of sources. But early on, I found that you learn best from writers who just happened to write about writing. I didn't learn much from people who made most of their living from writing texts and courses about writing. (Those books are inflated with redundant material that you've already learned. Most every book I've read like that could be summated into one or two pages of text.) The rest is all practice. And I wrote years of non-fiction before I moved to fiction. Often two or more blog posts per day, averaging about 2-4K words each. I also ran many of my short stories through ProWritingAid as an editor. (Once I did hire an editor for a non-fiction book. I learned what I needed from her. And I even followed the complex system of Shawn Coyne's Story Grid for months.) The end result was to quit all the courses when I stopped learning. And threw it all away after I'd internalized and practiced what they said as I tested it all. What tested out and aligned, I kept. This all led me to a study of the truly prolific fiction writers – the Pulp Golden Age writers, as well as the ones who came after them. And those commonalities pushed most of what passes for conventional writer's "wisdom" right out the window. (I have a book coming out, slated for December, where I'll re-compile all this actually useful data based on my year of prolific writing.)

Reading what I love, writing what I love – this I touched on above. You have to be very happy with what you write, every time you read it. A lot of people get behind this concept of "building an avatar" of your ideal customer. For the writer, fiction or non-fiction, it's far more personal. You write for yourself. You are your ideal customer. Don't let anyone kid you. There is no "writing to market." You are your best market. Whatever you love to read is the stuff you'll end up writing. And if you don't love what you write, neither will anyone else. Read widely, watch long-running TV series and serials. That's where you'll learn how to keep long story arcs going. People today expect that type of entertainment. Provide it – by providing it to yourself, first. You're going to attract people who like your writing as much as you do. Those are your first 1,000 true fans.

Making each book better than the last – most of this year was simply working out how to get my inspiration trained and work-flows ironed out. I didn't start out with really long stories, and I did scrounge up all the unpublished short fiction works I had written at any time. Studying these gave me what I needed to improve on. Only in the last couple of months have I gotten into writing real serials. Before that, I've been working simply on being able to write single-standing books. The last two weeks were set up for learning how to frame these books into serials, which is how story stories bridge to longer novels and story arcs.

Studying perennial-selling books – ignore the also-rans. Theodore Sturgeon stated a near-universal truth: "90% of everything out there is crud." While he was speaking of Science Fiction, it's very applicable to the bulk of the books being produced in any and every generation. Look up Louis L'Amour, Max Brand, Arthur Conan Doyle, and others. These books continue to sell and get downloaded regardless. Gutenburg.org has lists of these that have gone into the public domain. Those are the ones to dissect, emulate, internalize. There are huge numbers of current "bestsellers" who won't be selling in a few years – unless someone is keeping them advertised constantly.

Love what you read, write what you love – and you'll publish for the ages.

Summary: Where To From Here?

NOW YOU'VE GOT SOME real choices.

Writing short fiction or non-fiction is a simple way to get started and perfect your craft. And maybe get some pin-money or serious income along the way.

Combining your short works into longer collections and anthologies allows you to find readers who want the value of longer works. Longer works also allow you to create print versions that have a better chance of selling (with higher royalties than ebooks).

I've also touched on how to take that digital version of your book-content and transmogrify it into other versions and so get additional sales.

But nothing will happen until you slice out some regular time to write daily.

It doesn't matter how *much* you write as much as it matters *that* you write.

After you've been in the practice of writing at a particular time and in a particular space, then all these become habitual for you. And writing becomes second-nature.

As I complete this book, it's just under 7,000 words and I started it this morning before breakfast and then came back to it after lunch.

Of course, it's non-fiction. But I can tell you after three years that my fiction writing is the same. Sit down. Turn all other distractions off. Write.

It can be that simple for you, too.

But you have to start.

Of course, I've included additional books I've written if you need more advice in that area. Aren't you lucky? You're welcome

Until next time, then. Happy Writing!

Really Simple Writing & Publishing Series

———

BY DR. ROBERT C. WORSTELL

How I Survived My First Year of Fiction Writing[1]

How to Stop Feeding the Beast[2]

Author Freedom Guidebook[3]

Writing-Publishing Survival Guide[4]

Backwards Book Publishing: Save Time, Earn More, Work Less[5]

How to Write and Publish FOR FREE[6]

Cracking the Kindle Sales Code[7]

Really Simple Writing & Publishing[8]

An Honest Kindle Booksales Blueprint[9]

How to Help Librarians Love Your Book[10]

---

1. https://calm.li/FIrstYearFiction

2. https://calm.li/FeedingTheBeast

3. https://calm.li/AuthorFreedom

4. https://calm.li/PublishingSurvival

5. https://calm.li/BackwardsBookPub

6. https://calm.li/PublishForFree

7. https://calm.li/CrackingKindle

8. https://calm.li/ReallySimpleWP

9. https://calm.li/KindleBlueprint

10. https://calm.li/LibrariansLove

How to Write Less and Profit More[11]

Publish. Profit. Independence.[12]

J'APE: Just Another Publicity Excuse[13]

Writing Serial Fiction in the Real World[14]

11. https://calm.li/WriteLessProfitMore

12. https://calm.li/2mG93LW

13. https://calm.li/JAPE

14. https://calm.li/WritingSerialFiction

Becoming A Writer Series

―――――

BECOMING A WRITER[1]

This Fiction Business[2]

Mystery Story Techniques for Writers[3]

Learning from the Pulp Masters[4]

How I Survived My First Year of Fiction Writing[5]

1. https://calm.li/BecomingAWriterBook

2. https://calm.li/ThisFictionBusiness

3. https://calm.li/MysteryStoryTechniques

4. https://calm.li/Pulp_Masters

5. https://calm.li/FIrstYearFiction

Becoming a Writer Courses

———

A SAMPLER OF OUR EXPANDING suite of courses:

Becoming A Writer -

Dorothea Brande's original classic worked up into a readily learnable series of lessons, along with related references for download to improve the experience...

Author Freedom Course -

That which begins well, goes well. Learn the simple steps to acquire real freedom in your writing and publishing. A very frank and simple series of steps so you can get started today – with only what you already have at hand.

Backwards Book Publishing -

Books, in all their versions, are idea containers. The trick to leveraging these is to work backward from the most profitable container, the non-fiction course...

How to Write Less, Profit More -

How writing short stories – a traditional starting place for many writers – enables you to learn your craft faster, and create more outlets for income meanwhile...

———

https://livesensical.com/go/becomingawritercourses/

Did You Like This Book?

————

HOW ABOUT LEAVING A review with the vendor?

Otherwise (or in addition) you can leave your recommendations on:

- **Bookbub**[1]

The whole point is to enable others to find books that you liked reading.

Which then helps you find more great books to read.

And...

Feel free to share this book!

---

1. https://www.bookbub.com/recommendations

Did you love *How to Write Less and Profit More - Version 2.0*? Then you should read *How I Survived My First Year of Fiction Writing*[2] by Dr. Robert C. Worstell!

HOW I SURVIVED MY FIRST YEAR OF FICTION WRITING

DR. ROBERT C. WORSTELL [3]

Writing Fiction isn't very hard - *if you throw out 95% of what you've been taught is true.*

Academics and those who earn their income marketing how-to books and courses, as well as freelance editors, proofreaders, and cover designers all have a vested interest in making it seem that writing and publishing is very difficult.

It's just not true at all.

Yes, there is a lot of hard work to it. And it's not something you can learn overnight. And you have to keep studying and practicing your craft to get any good at it - just as musicians and athletes practice daily.

2. https://books2read.com/u/bO6EyW

3. https://books2read.com/u/bO6EyW

But you can publish your first book on Amazon in a half hour from now. It's that simple. (Of course you can use a pen name to avoid being embarassed later.)

The point is that writing and publishing is simple, and inexpensive.

Here's the secret: **Write short and narrow, publish long and wide.**

Write short stories for a specific sub-genre you like to read.

Publish long in advance (pre-schedule) and wide to every possible outlet - including free ones like Wattpad and Medium.

Including setting up all the accounts, you can publish everywhere on the globe in an afternoon. For no cost, except your time.

This book is a compilation of the blog posts I wrote and published while I was busy doing a test of everything I'd rounded up and studied about writing and publishing fiction.

And it's a very raw, passionate description of exactly what I found works - as I was testing it.

So it's more an adventure that starts from having no published fiction and ends up with have well over a hundred books published. Step by step, blow by blow.

To test what I'd found and bring it all to you.

Scroll Up and Get Your Copy Now.

Read more at https://livesensical.com/book-author/dr-robert-c-worstell/.

Also by Dr. Robert C. Worstell

Change Your Life Toolset
Get Your Self Scam Free

Make Yourself Great Again Library
Why You Got All That Stuff
The Art of Wonk, Compleat

Masters of Copywriting
Breakthrough Copywriter 2.0: An Advertising Field Guide to Eugene
M. Schwartz' Classic

Mindset Stacking Guides
Make Yourself Great Again Part 1
Make Yourself Great Again Part 2
Make Yourself Great Again Part 3
Make Yourself Great Again Part 4
Choose. Believe. Win.
Make Yourself Great Again - Complete Collection

Go Thunk Yourself, Again!

PMA Science of Success
Napoleon Hill's PMA: Science of Success Course - An Introduction

Really Simple Writing & Publishing
How To Write And Publish For Free
Backwards Book Publishing: Save Time, Earn More, Work Less
Writing-Publishing Survival Guide
Author Freedom Guidebook
How to Stop Feeding the Beast
A Completely Unauthorized Instafreebie Guidebook
How I Survived My First Year of Fiction Writing
How to Become an Instant Author in 30 Seconds
Becoming a Wealthy Writer
Marketers & Writers - Scammers & Dupes
How to Write Less and Profit More - Version 2.0

Standalone
Farm Less, Profit More: Lessons in Regenerative Grazing

Watch for more at https://livesensical.com/book-author/
dr-robert-c-worstell/.

Midwest Journal Press
Finding You Books that Continue to Change Your Life

About the Publisher

"Finding you books that continue to change your life."

A veteran publishing imprint and a practical philosophy for life, Midwest Journal Press has been active publishing new and established authors since 2006.

We take advantage of the new Print on Demand and ebook technologies to enable wider discovery for authors.

We publish in most of the major genres of fiction and non-fiction.

Our current emphasis is in speculative fiction modern parables.

For More Information, Visit:

https://livesensical.com/midwestjournalpress/